Little Artist

A Childs Art Book

By CHARACTER BUILDERS FOR Kids

Art
as seen
through the
eyes of
a child...

This book belongs to

_____

Age _____

This is me

This is my home

This is my family

This is my best friend

This is someone who makes me feel special

This is my teacher

This is what I want to be when I grow up

This is a pet I would like to have

Little Artist Signature

Little Artist Signature

Little Artist Signature

Little Artist Signature

Little Artist Signature

Little Artist Signature

Little Artist Signature

Little Artist Signature

Little Artist Signature

Little Artist Signature

Little Artist Signature

Little Artist Signature

Little Artist Signature

Little Artist Signature

Little Artist Signature

Little Artist Signature

Little Artist Signature

Little Artist Signature